Only He Can Change Your Story

*When the World Calls You a Victim,
God Calls You Victorious*

Capri Prentice

Only He Can Change Your Story: When the World Calls You a Victim, God Calls You Victorious / Capri Prentice. —1st edition.

ISBN: 979-8-9991792-0-3

To my three wildly amazing boys
who always keep me on my toes,
and my husband, whose fault it is that
I am a forever boy mom.
Love you more!

Contents

Only He Can
Change Your Story

Preface

You are the light of the world—like a city on a hilltop that cannot be hidden. No one lights a lamp and then puts it under a basket. Instead, a lamp is placed on a stand, where it gives light to everyone in the house. In the same way, let your good deeds shine out for all to see, so that everyone will praise your heavenly Father.

—Matthew 5:14–16

I struggled to write this book over five years. I repeatedly put off writing, talking myself out of it so many times by thinking, "Who am I to write a book? I am terrible at spelling and grammar. I am not qualified to write anything, let alone publish a book. Why would someone want to read about my experience?" The worry about who would read my story, what they would think, and how I could clearly portray what I wanted to say kept me in a holding pattern for years. I blamed my lack of progress on not having the time or being too busy with my full-time job, ministry, and raising three boys, but really, pride was getting in my way. I delayed writing time and time again until I stopped altogether for about two years. Then God stepped in. I realized the story I wanted to write was not just about me. In the Book of Revelation, the writer, John the Revelator, addresses how the faithful saints conquered the enemy by the blood of the Lamb and the word of their testimony. Their testimony. If we silence our testimony and keep it to ourselves, we rob others of their opportunity to overcome. We can't know the power our testimony might have in someone else's life unless we share it.

This book is not just about my story. It's about God's amazing love, grace, and forgiveness. It's about what He wants to say through my story, how He wants to reveal who He is, and who He wants to connect with and completely change. God wants to help us have victory over hardships we may be facing. We don't have to accept the hand we were dealt. We do not have to live in constant fear, anger, hurt, rejection, betrayal or pain. Jesus paid the price to give us victory here on Earth. If we keep silent about what God has done in our lives, others may never get the opportunity to truly experience the God we know.

After about five years of painstakingly slow progress, I finally got God's message loud and clear. "I have done an amazing thing in your life, and I want you to share it to help others break out of the bondage and pain they have had for years. But if you choose not to use this gift I gave you, I'll

move on and use someone else." That was the wake-up call I needed! I remembered a phrase I'd heard from our pastors at the time: *Delayed obedience is still disobedience.* Talk about conviction—phew! God wanted to use me to bring freedom to others, and He wants to use you, too. But this mission has a time limit. Jesus is coming soon. There is an urgency in the call that warrants us to respond.

So, I did what I should have done from the start: I sought accountability for what I needed to accomplish. I reached out to a few amazing women who knew my testimony. They encouraged me to write and be obedient to the last thing that God told me to do. Then I got bolder and told a group of women at church about my long-held secret: I was writing a book. I couldn't run away from or delay my assignment any longer. It was time. I looked for the rare times I didn't have a million things going on to write. I would sit down with a large cup of coffee and ask the Lord, *What do you want me to say? What do your people need to hear from me?* I asked those questions because I found that when I put my own thoughts and desires on the back burner and asked God for His way, the results were always better than what I could do myself.

As I wrote, I was always conscious that I did not want to cause any feelings of shame in those who are still hurting. Healing is a process, and we are all at different stages of forgiveness and healing. The mission of this book is to let you know that there is hope and that Jesus brings freedom. This is something that only He can do. I will tell you truthfully that I do not have it all figured out. I still need reminders from the

Holy Spirit to forgive when people hurt me. I am flawed, but the word of God is not.

You'll notice I reference scriptures frequently in my writing. The only place to find truth, lasting impact, and change comes from the life-giving power revealed in the Word of God—not a person's opinions or experience but God's truth. Maybe you are going through a trial right now, and a dear friend gave you this book. Let the Word of God be a life-giving source to your weary heart. As you read, I encourage you to spend time with these scriptures. Read them, highlight them in your Bible, meditate on them, and allow them to impact and change you. Scripture is not merely words on a page but the very real and active words of the living God who loves you. These scriptures have the power to change you from the inside out if you allow them to. I pray my story will shine a spotlight inward for every reader to see areas they may need to reflect on, identify issues they may need to seek help for, and highlight matters in which they may need to enact change.

While I share terrible things that happened to me, the poor choices I made as a result, and the unforgiveness I harbored, out of all that comes my testimony of the power of God and how He completely changed my story, as only He can. The saddest part of my story is that it will be all too familiar to many readers. Let me reassure you: just because bad things happen to you, you do not need to let them define you. No matter your current level of relationship with God— whether you are in daily communion or in a state of unbe-

4

lief—if you go on this journey with me, I believe your life will be positively impacted and prayerfully changed.

Hold on for the ride!

And we know that God causes everything to work together for the good of those who love God and are called according to his purpose for them.

—Romans 8:28

I pray that you will find healing from a past hurt, situation, circumstance, or any other evil that happened to you. I pray that through reading these pages, you experience the full love of God and develop the desire to know Him more. You are not the sum of the things that have happened to you: you are a new creation in Christ and *more* than a conqueror.

The world may have called you a victim, but God calls you victorious.

God Knows You,
Loves You,
Cares for You,
and God Is Good

"For I know the plans that I have for you,"
*says the L*ORD*. "They are plans for good and*
not for disaster, to give you a future and a
hope."

—*Jeremiah 29:11*

G od knew you before you were put in your mother's
womb: He formed you and has big plans for you. God
has a plan to prosper you and not to harm you. You are not
an accident, and you are not a mistake. God created you for a
specific purpose and has the best plans for your life.

There are some things that we need to clear up about
who God is. People generally do a very poor job of explain-
ing who God is based on their individual life circumstanc-

es. God is not a god based on our circumstances. He is God based on the truth found in His Word. There are many misconceptions about God in the world; unfortunately, there are even misconceptions about God in the church.

First and foremost, God does not cause bad things to happen to us. God is a good father who only wants good things for His children. He loves all His creation, calls it all good, and only wants the absolute best for us.

> *Every good gift and every perfect gift is from above, and comes down from the Father of lights, with whom there is no variation or shadow of turning.*
>
> *—James 1:17 NKJV*

We do have an enemy. Scripture refers to him by many names. One is *the thief.* He hates God and hates us because we were made in the image of God. But he especially loves when the very creation God loves and made blames God for things the thief is responsible for.

> *The thief comes only to steal and kill and destroy. I came that they may have life and have it abundantly.*
>
> *—John 10:10 ESV*

Bad things happen in a fallen world. To the amazement of many, God does not control everything. Yes, I said it: God does not control everything. For example, He cannot control

our free will. Free will is the best and worst gift God ever gave us. We have the ability to choose to do good or choose to do evil. We can choose to follow our own plans or choose to follow God's. The evil things a person chooses to do are not a result of God's will or His fault. Often, we blame God for something He had no part in. The consequences of some of the choices we (or others) make can end in the opposite of God's original intentions.

In the Garden of Eden, there was perfection. God created Eden to show us His will: there was no sin there, no hurt, no bloodshed, and Adam and Eve had a full relationship with God. Genesis 3:8 shows Adam walking with God in the cool of the day. Unfortunately, humanity chose to sin and disobey God, separating us from Him. It says in Genesis that God gave us dominion over all the Earth, but when we sinned, we gave that dominion to the devil (the lowercase "god" of this world). God has always given us the choice to choose Him or not to choose Him. If we choose not to follow Him, we actually choose to be the god of our own lives and thus follow the god of this world, who is Satan. As the scripture above shows, he only has evil intentions for our lives. The thief, or Satan, comes only to steal, kill, and destroy. Adam and Eve's decision not to obey God led to the broken world we now live in. This was the original sin. Adam and Eve, man and woman, humanity, had everything—they were created in the very image of God—and yet they chose to disobey. They chose to allow the lies of that serpent to deceive them into thinking they were lacking. Today, we still have free will, and we can

choose the lies of the enemy or the truth of God.

Another common misconception is that God lets bad things happen to us to teach us a lesson.

But God is Love.

> *So we have come to know and to believe the love that God has for us. God is love, and whoever abides in love abides in God, and God abides in him.*
>
> —*1 John 4:16 ESV*

God is all good, all love, and all righteousness. He does not wish terrible things to happen to anyone. God calls you His beloved, His child. No good parent wants anything bad to happen to their child or would intentionally harm them.

> *You parents—if your children ask for a loaf of bread, do you give them a stone instead? Or if they ask for a fish, do you give them a snake? Of course not! So if you sinful people know how to give good gifts to your children, how much more will your heavenly Father give good gifts to those who ask him.*
>
> —*Matthew 7:9–11*

God does not want evil things to happen to you, and He would not put terrible things on you to teach you a lesson. That is the total opposite of His character, which we

see time and time again in the Bible. He can, however, take what the devil intended to harm and destroy you and make it into a testimony that can show how amazing God is. He can heal you of all past hurt and offense. He can free you from years of pain, fear, anxiety and heartache. What the enemy meant to use to harm you and break you can become the brightest light in your story, and it can help others break free. That is what only our God can do!

God is Still Good—Above it All

God is not a man, so He does not lie.
He is not human, so He does not change
His mind.
Has He ever spoken and failed to act?
Has He ever promised and not carried it
through?

—Numbers 23:19

What I want you to take away is that God is good through it all. He never changes. He was there before the beginning, and He will be there forever. His character does not change, and His promises do not change. He cannot lie. He is always faithful and always good. He will never leave or forsake us, no matter what we go through or may face. He is there with us *through* it all. That is amazing to me and so reassuring. We don't have to do it alone.

> *The LORD rescues the godly;*
>   *he is their fortress in times of trouble.*
>
> —*Psalm 37:39*

A life of faith does not mean a life free of pain, but God is there for you, even in the midst of life's biggest storms. He is like a strong tower protecting you on all sides.

> *The LORD directs the steps of the godly.*
>   *He delights in every detail of their lives.*
> *Though they stumble, they will never fall,*
>   *for the LORD holds them by the hand.*
> *Once I was young, and now I am old.*
>   *Yet I have never seen the godly abandoned...*
>
> *Psalm 37:23–25*

He will never abandon us. He delights in every detail of our lives. Nothing is too big or too small for God. People may hurt, leave, or abandon us, but God never will. He is there through it all, and He will never fail us.

Don't Believe the Lies

So often, we try to hide the negative things that happen in our lives. The enemy wants us to hold onto the shame of trauma and hurt. He wants us to feel isolated and victim to whatever happened to us. The label *victim* can be debilitating. It's like a suit of armor we wear to keep experiences and people out. We think we need to protect ourselves when,

in reality, we need God and other people to help build us up. The devil knows that if we are alone and feel like no one can understand, we will never seek help for the things we struggle with. We will not seek healing from the pain that has been silently eating away at us for years. If we are isolated in shame, the enemy can continually keep feeding us little lies meant to break us. When we are alone in our pain, we are vulnerable, and we start to believe the voice inside that says, "Maybe I could have done something to prevent that; maybe I had it coming; maybe this is what I deserve." But these are lies straight from hell itself.

It's worth repeating: the things that have happened to you are not the things that have to define you.

For years, I did not want to talk about what happened to me. I felt like I shouldn't or couldn't talk about it. I desperately wanted to preserve a picturesque ideal of being in a perfect Christian family. However, bad things can happen—even in a good home. The enemy works hard to try to isolate us. He wants to label us as victims and make defeat and shame our final story. He does not want us to know there is hope, complete healing, and forgiveness through Jesus. He does not want us to know we can have joy again and a story of victory out of what most would consider our darkest times.

But God has given me *exactly* that outcome! He turned what the enemy meant for evil into an amazing testimony of His goodness, unfailing love, and forgiveness. I now know I don't have to be ashamed of what happened to me, and I have

13

learned God's awesome love and power cannot be revealed unless we open our mouths and tell others about the things God has done for us.

> *And they overcame him because of the blood*
> *of the Lamb and because of the word of their*
> *testimony.*
>
> —*Revelation 12:11 NASB*

This book is not meant to compare my situation with yours or what awful things happened to you or someone you love. It is not meant to glorify a person or a situation or put anything on an unobtainable pedestal. I am simply telling my story about how God helped change my story. I know He wants to help you, too, through your past or current hurt. I write to remind you He is good through it all.

There is no place or reason to compare stories. There is no reason to feel your pain is insignificant just because it's not as bad of a situation that others have faced. Any hurt or pain you face is not God's plan for you. *Everyone* deserves to be loved and taken care of. *No one* deserves to be abused or taken advantage of. Whatever happened to you was *wrong*. If you are currently facing a situation of abuse or torment, I pray you are empowered to break free. You are worthy of love, respect and healing.

From Hurt to Healed

Healing is a process. With God's help, it can be a quick process for some. For others, it takes longer. Part of the process of being healed involves forgiving those who've hurt us. Saying we want to forgive someone does not make what they did okay or justify their actions; it simply says that we won't hold on to the hurt they've caused anymore. We give the hurt to the One who can take it away and give us complete healing and peace.

I had to realize that the things that happened to me were wrong, they were not my fault, and I could not have prevented them. This realization let me come to a place where I could forgive myself. That often is a huge first step and a place where many people can get tripped up and delay their healing. I had to know that I was worth getting my healing (more about that later).

Secular advisors may teach a similar message—that the abuse was not our fault. But then we may be left to try to fit the broken pieces back together alone. Worldly wisdom will tell us that we can hurt for a while, but after that, we must move on. The options we are given may include medicating the pain away, going to therapy to learn to live with anger, fear, or anxiety, or trying self-help techniques so that the memory won't haunt us. Worst of all, we may reject all advice and keep our anger and hate tucked inside. None of these are lasting solutions. They are merely Band-Aids and not very strong ones. We're left silently clinging to pain because these options do not bring healing. They only diffuse,

delay, or temporarily bury the pain. They put the determining factor of healing totally on you, but there are many things we are not capable of doing on our own.

In the past, I felt like I was not strong enough to deal with what happened to me. I would wonder why I couldn't just push it down and sweep it away far enough not to have to feel it anymore. I tried to deny it, numb it, self-medicate it, hide it, and lock it away, but these were all just quick fixes that never worked for long.

We may be able to return to some sense of normalcy for a time, but eventually, our feelings will take root and bitterness, anger, hate, unforgiveness, shame, and a lack of self-worth will build up. Such deadly roots will kill any hope, joy or love in our lives and continue ruining future relationships—not just worldly ones. The Bible talks about how unforgiveness hinders your relationship with God (more on that later).

God is the only one who can bring us total and complete healing. We are not meant to do it on our own. The Word talks about *sozo* healing. *Sozo* means "to save, deliver, protect, heal, preserve, and make whole." God can take something horrible that we've let define us for so long and make it feel like it isn't even our story—not because we deny it happened, but because He literally can take the pain associated with it away. Only God can do that! Therapy and medication can numb and hide pain for a time, but they cannot heal.

There is only one Healer.

He heals the brokenhearted
And binds up their wounds.

　　　　　　　　　—Psalm 147:3 NASB

My Story—
Innocence Taken

I grew up in a loving home. My parents worked at my school and in ministry. If someone was in need, they were the ones to help. The school would reach out to my parents if troubled children needed a safe place to stay. Many kids came to our home for a night, a week, a month, or more.

When I was nine years old, a boy named Dean came to live with us. He was removed from his biological father's home because of serious abuse. Dean had been living with my family for about six months when Dean's mom began talking about giving up her parental rights, and my parents began the process of looking into adoption. He became like a brother, attending family gatherings, Sunday church services, and family vacations. He was one of the family.

But in just one night, everything changed.

My parents left the house for a few hours while my older siblings and I stayed home. I remember being with my sister and Dean that evening. We were sitting on the couch with an old scratchy grey blanket over us, watching *The Wild*

Thornberrys. It was summertime, too warm for a blanket. But I didn't take it off when Dean put it over us. Dean touched my leg under the blanket. I was confused. What was he doing? His hand slowly went up to my shorts. It didn't stop. He continued up, and as his hand went up my shirt, I froze in terror. His hands touched my chest and made me so uncomfortable as a 9-year-old girl who was still embarrassed by the changes of a growing body. I sat there stunned as he eventually moved his hands down to unbutton my shorts and touch me in ways no child should be touched. I was scared and shocked by what was happening but didn't move. I couldn't. I glanced toward him out of the corner of my eye. He was looking straight forward—like nothing was happening. At one point, I looked over in horror to make sure he wasn't also touching my sister, who was sitting on the other side of him. He didn't stop—it went on through the entire grueling TV episode. I did not know what to do. When would it stop? I felt helpless.

When the show was finally over, I was paralyzed. I sat on the couch in a daze, like I was in a terrible dream. I next felt Dean take me by the hand towards the stairs leading down to his room. I screamed inside, but no sound came out. I didn't want to go with him. I didn't want any of this to happen. I didn't know what would happen next or when it would end.

The moment my feet touched the top of the first stair, my parents got home. It was like a jolt that I desperately needed to shake me out of the horrible nightmare I was in. I ran to my bedroom and pretended to be asleep. I cried myself to

sleep that night, not understanding what had happened or why. I was haunted by the feeling that his hands were still on me. The thought that Dean might appear in my room at any minute terrorized me throughout the night.

I lost all sense of control and safety in my own home.

***

The days after the event are a blur. I tried not to think about what happened and tried desperately to forget, but every time I tried, I would continue to feel Dean's hands on my little body again and feel dirty, ashamed, and confused. I avoided him at any cost and could not make eye contact. I wanted it all to go away. I wanted to pretend like it never happened. Every night, I went to bed, fearing that maybe that night would be the night his figure would come into my room and do who knows what. The thought terrorized me. I did not get much sleep in the days that followed.

After what felt like a lifetime, but it was probably only about a week, my mom was getting ready to pick up my sister from play practice on a Saturday morning. The school was only about a 15-minute drive, round trip, and my mom was not planning to be gone for long. I don't remember why, but I said, "I want to go, too."

Mom was in a rush. She asked me to stay home, saying, "I'll only be gone for a few minutes." She reassured me my older siblings were there, including Dean, and said, "You'll be fine."

My heart raced as I firmly protested and followed her to

the minivan. I jumped in before she could tell me to just stay home again.

I had always been clingy as a child. My mom loves to tell stories about how I would not let her out of my sight as a baby. Even if she went into the next room, I would cry. But that day was different. Mom has since told me she recalls something or someone telling her not to just pass off my behavior as part of my normal clingy, stubborn nature but to ask why I was so adamant about coming.

Still parked in the driveway, Mom asked, "Why can't you stay home?"

I vaguely remember avoiding eye contact with her in the rearview mirror while saying something about not wanting to stay with Dean.

Mom replied, "But he is asleep downstairs." She turned around to face me and pushed for more information. She could tell something was wrong.

My heartbeat was in my throat, and I tried to hold back my tears. I was tired as I had been pushing all my emotions down and pretending like nothing had happened for days. But at that moment, looking into my mom's eyes, I couldn't take it anymore. The dam burst. Tears ran down my little face, and I told my mom what had happened that night and how I was afraid that it might happen again.

My mom's facial expression quickly changed from annoyed to sheer panic. She told me to stay in the van. She quickly went and got everyone else out of the house and ushered them into the van while Dean was still asleep. My

siblings were reluctant and didn't understand why they had to wake up early on a Saturday morning to get in the car. Mom didn't tell them why. She simply said, "You all just need to come now."

She drove us to a family friend's house while she called my dad to decide what to do next. My siblings and I were sent upstairs to play. I snuck away from them and peered down over the top of the stair rail to listen. I had never seen my mom so panicked. She was trying to think of a plan and think logically, all while shattering inside. It was one of the first times I ever saw my mom break down and weep with our family friends. I felt so sorry and ashamed. The question of why this happened must have been running through her head while she probably fought off wicked thoughts of blaming herself. Now that I'm a parent, I still cannot imagine everything she must have felt.

We were taken to my grandparents' home next. The other kids watched a movie while I sat with my mom, dad, grandmother, and grandfather at the dining room table. The table was always one of my favorite places to be as a child. It was filled with memories of the room packed for Thanksgiving dinners, competitive card games, and sitting around listening to stories from relatives, but that day was very different. That day, everyone's faces revealed a mix of anguish, anger and pity. Sitting at the table where I'd always felt comfortable, warm, and loved, I suddenly felt small and distant. With sunken faces, my parents told me Dean would no longer be living with us. He had to leave. Right then.

The whole room seemed to come crashing down. I was shocked and instantly regretted telling my mom. While I didn't know the full extent of Dean's background, I knew he did not come from a good, loving home. I didn't know if he would have to go back there or someplace worse. I knew my family provided love and stability for him. Now, because I told what had happened, that would be taken away from him. I knew he was broken and needed a family, but now he would not have that, all because of me. The enemy would re-play this lie over and over again in my mind: *I took the chance of having a loving family away from him.* This guilt consumed me in later years and made me hate myself. *It's all my fault.*

I wanted to take it all back. I thought to myself, *I never would have told Mom if I knew this would be the result.* I cried to my parents, "Isn't there something else we can do?" But when we got home that night, Dean and all his things were gone. I never saw him again in that house. The person who hurt me was gone, but the wounds that he left remained en-trenched in me.

The Aftermath

I was sent to therapy shortly after because this is what the world tells us to do. "Go see someone and talk about it." I *hated* therapy. The therapist kept urging me to talk about what happened repeatedly. As a child therapist, she wanted me to draw how I felt about what happened, do play therapy scenarios with toys in similar situations, write a letter, and other seemingly strange techniques to my little nine-year-old

self that were supposed to help me heal. To me, therapy sessions felt like reliving the experience over and over again. I would remember how his hands felt on me, touching me all over, and the panic I felt like I was right back on that couch. I just wanted it to stop!

The same message was repeated at the end of each session: "It's not your fault." The common theme was that I was the victim and that I couldn't blame myself for what happened to me. But deep down, I did blame myself. I blamed myself for talking about what happened that night and causing Dean to lose the loving, caring place he needed. I even blamed myself for not stopping it from happening in the first place. I blamed myself and thought maybe I did or said something to make him think it was okay to touch me or that I wanted him to, when in reality, I still didn't truly understand what had happened.

The memory of it replayed over and over again in my mind. I kept going through all the things that I wished I could have or should have done but, in the moment, couldn't. I kept hearing the voice in my head saying, "You could have stopped it. You could have said no. It's your fault!" The voice never faded—it got louder and stronger as the years passed.

But I now recognize whose voice it was and its purpose—to steal, kill, and destroy.

***

After everything happened, I had many nightmares. I became the very victim that my therapist spoke of. I took

on that persona. I was afraid of Dean and of what was happening to him. I had dreams about Dean being locked up in a dark prison somewhere, hating me for causing him to be kicked out of our home. I was afraid of what he would do to me if he ever saw me again and convinced he probably hated me for ruining his chance at a better life.

Many years passed. I eventually suppressed my feelings, and the nightmares faded, but I carried the weight of being a victim. I felt like the word was tattooed on my forehead. As the years passed and I grew into a teenager, I began a long battle with self-destructive actions stemming from a lack of self-worth. Drinking, taking drugs, having sex, engaging with eating disorders and whatever else helped me feel numb or made me feel better, even temporarily, were normal vices. I justified my behaviors with the logic that since I was the victim, I deserved to feel broken, I deserved to act how I wanted to, and I deserved to be angry. I wanted to blame everything on Dean and what he did to me.

I should be depressed and hate myself. I should want to end my life. I should have body issues and want to cut or starve myself. I AM THE VICTIM! I deserve to feel like this and act like this. I am justified.

At some point, everything changed, and I no longer worried about Dean. I hated him. I hated what my life had become and blamed it on what he did to me. *He made me a victim*, I thought, *and if I am going to be a victim, then I am going to live it up as much as possible.* I was going to do anything that I wanted to do to feel better. I drank with the end

goal of blacking out to numb what I was feeling. I used sex as a weapon that I could control with someone, anyone, to feel worth something. But the deeper I dug my hole of being the victim, the harder it was to get out.

I not only ran from God, I sprinted in the other direction. I wanted to believe that He was not there or was not real, that a God so powerful would not let something so awful happen to me. I'd been a good kid. I tried to be nice to people and care for others. I went to church every Sunday, said my prayers before bed, and sometimes read my kids' Bible. So how could a good God let something so evil happen to me? I came to want to believe God was just something that my parents brainwashed me into believing when I was a child and that they only believed in Him because they were weak-minded, uneducated followers who could not face reality. But deep down, hidden away, I knew better. I knew God was real. I had felt His presence and seen Him do things that no one could explain or do.

My senior year and beyond were filled with a darkness that is hard to explain. There was an emptiness within me. Everything inside me felt shattered, while outside, I looked like I had everything together. I was good at masking my brokenness. I was a straight-A student, excelled in sports and music, and was friends with just about everyone—but none of that mattered. I didn't know who I was anymore, so I would morph to fit into whatever peer group I was around. At this dark point, God was almost a laughable subject to me. I was not serving the Lord or even acknowledging His

existence. I just wanted to feel better by any means possible. I tried to replace my hurt and anger with anything that felt good, no matter how temporal. I accepted anything as okay and accepted anyone's influence and advice on how to help me heal. By trying to fix myself and numb my feelings, I was creating a bigger sense of worthlessness within. I was causing a great separation of who I was and whose I was.

You see, we can choose. I chose to turn away from God through this time in my life. I chose to self-medicate and do my own thing. God gave us free will—which is the best (and worst!) gift ever. He cannot go against our free will. He is a gentleman, and if we slam the door repeatedly and tell Him to leave, He will respect our request. But He is never far off.

The Spiral

Why can I not fix this myself? Am I not strong enough? I need to get over it! It's not like it was really that bad; it's not like he raped me. It only happened that one time. It could have been worse. Other people have worse things happen, and they seem okay.

I told myself such things to try to make my feelings of worthlessness and of being the victim go away. But they never did.

In college, everything came to a head. I was free from the standards and expectations I had as a high school student and out from under the watchful eyes of people who cared about me—my parents, teachers, and coaches. With my new-

found freedom, I made disastrous choices. I fell into a spiral of drugs, weekly blackouts, stealing, more sexual partners than I can remember, encounters with the police, suicidal depression and even deeper feelings of loneliness and worthlessness.

I felt like I could not talk to my family. I was ashamed of how far away I had gone and knew what I was doing was wrong. I didn't think they would understand my pain. I would lie to myself that what I was going through and my drinking was just a typical college experience. *This is normal, right?* No—it wasn't normal not to remember anything that happened the night before. It wasn't normal to walk around campus, afraid to lift my head because I didn't know if I would see someone I had hooked up with and never spoken to again. It wasn't normal to see my friends only on nights and weekends, not during the week. I was trying to suppress all sense of right and wrong. I told myself, *It's because I'm a victim and this is what happens—this is how victims deal with what happened.* But deep down, I hated myself: I hated everything about me. I struggled with suicidal thoughts and made multiple attempts.

I hit my lowest point during my senior year of college. It was New Year's Eve, 2012. I was back home from college on winter break, and instead of being with family, I chose to go out with friends. I went to a party and completely blacked out. It wasn't a new experience. To this day, I still have no idea what happened. I blacked back in to find myself crawling backward up a flight of stairs on my hands while kicking

at some girls to fight them off from beating me up. I reached the top of the stairs and locked myself in a room. I could hear the girls pounding on the door and screaming at me. I had no idea who they were, where I was, or why they were screaming. I was terrified.

Somehow, through my drunken daze, I realized I had my phone and managed to call a number. It was about 2:00 am. Through drunk, double vision, I saw the name on the screen of the number I called. Mom. I screamed into the phone repeatedly, "You need to come get me!" I didn't have a lot of details I could give her other than that I was in a college town, and I'd locked myself in an upstairs room somewhere near downtown. By the grace of God, my parents found me. My mom will tell you that she still has no idea how she was able to navigate the maze of that college town and find the exact house I was in, but God had his hand in it all.

As a result of that night, I lost everyone and everything I cared about at the time. I could no longer hide how lost I was from my family or how bad my drinking had gotten. None of my friends would talk to me anymore. They no longer asked me to come drink with them, which was my only social activity. Even my college housemates despised me. When I walked into the room, they acted like I wasn't there. Who could blame them? I shut everyone and everything out. I pushed everyone away and built a huge wall between me and the world. I hurt people, slept around, said terrible things, lied, stole, cheated, and backstabbed. I didn't care about anyone or anything. I was fully submerged in my sin, and it was

choking the life out of me. I didn't want to live anymore. I felt alone and surrounded by darkness all the time. I knew what I was doing wasn't right, and I thought, *There's no way God could still love someone like me after all that I've done, after how far I've gone.*

I was shattered and lost. I had nothing left in me and nowhere to turn. But amid all the darkness, a still, small voice called me back to the One who had always been there.

God's Reversal

I was in the final semester of my final year of college and was sitting in my room, crying out to anything at that point because I was lost, alone, and hopeless, when I remembered I had an old Bible tucked away somewhere. When I was packing up to go to college the summer before my freshman semester, my dad had snuck it into one of my suitcases. I went to the closet. Under a pile of shoes was a dark green bin I hadn't opened since I moved in. In that bin was an old green Bible. I took it out. I looked at it with the pain of desperation, and I figured I had nothing else to lose.

> *Come close to God, and God will come close to you.*
>
> *—James 4:8*

God is a gentleman. He will not force you to love Him. He will not force Himself on you. This is free will. We can choose to try and do things our way and be the god of our lives, or we can choose to let God be God.

But God does not just sweep life away; instead, he devises ways to bring us back when we have been separated from Him.

—2 Samuel 14:14

No matter how far we run, hide, fight back, mock Him, or deny Him, He still does not wish anyone to be separated from Him. He is faithful and patient and forgives us when we turn to Him. We can never be too far gone. Nothing can separate us from the love of Christ.

And I am convinced that nothing can separate us from God's love. Neither death nor life, neither angels nor demons, neither our fears for today nor our worries about tomorrow— not even the powers of hell can separate us from God's love. No power in the sky above or in the earth below—indeed, nothing in all creation will ever be able to separate us from the love of God that is revealed in Christ Jesus our Lord.

—Romans 8:38–39

I finally was at the point where I cried out to God. I didn't even know if I truly believed He existed, but I figured I had nothing else to lose and nowhere else to turn. I began to weep as I sat on my bed and opened the Bible. This was my last chance. If I did not find the answer here, then I was done.

Done with everything.

I thought, *Maybe if I beg or do enough good things and try to be a really good person, God will forgive me. Maybe He will look past all that I've done.* I turned to what I thought was a random page. But God had led me to the parables of the lost sheep and the prodigal son in Luke chapter 15.

A Lost Sheep Found and the Prodigal Returned

What's remarkable about these parables is that they show God's love in all its fullness. The parable of the lost sheep illustrates how God will literally leave the 99 to go and search for the one: "And when he has found it, he will joyfully carry it home on his shoulders" (Luke 15:5). How wonderful that the one who runs off is carried back with joy! I felt the Lord say, "I will carry you." He leaves all the others to search for the one that has gone astray. He doesn't just leave them or get angry that they left, but He lovingly carries them back with joy. He is not ashamed and doesn't make them sneak in through the back. He shows His love and devotion by carrying the one who has gone astray close, showing that the lost sheep is His.

I kept reading. In the parable of the prodigal son, the son takes his inheritance from his father, goes far off and squanders it on unholy things. He makes such poor choices that he ends up all alone, sitting in a pig pen, hungry, dirty, and ashamed. But he remembers that even the servants in his father's house were treated better. He feels ashamed but says he will go back to his father's house: maybe his father will take

him back in as a servant. He doesn't think he is deserving of forgiveness or love again. But the Bible says, "And while he was still a long way off, his father saw him coming. Filled with love and compassion, he ran to his son, embraced him, and kissed him" (Luke 15:20). The father embraces his son, puts shoes on his feet, clothes him in a robe of honor and gives him a signet ring showing that this boy is his son.

Think about it: if the father saw his wayward son returning from a far way off—that means he was *looking* for him! The father never gave up hope that his son would return.

When the father sees the son, he is filled with compassion, not condemnation or anger. So joyful that his son has finally come home, the father runs to him. That is how God feels about us! The son only hopes to come back as a servant, but the father restores him to his place as a son. God loves you and me so much. Even in all my mess and sin, God said, "I still love you, and you are my child."

> ...*God clearly shows and proves His own love for us, by the fact that while we were still sinners, Christ died for us.*
>
> —*Romans 5:8 AMP*

Even in all my sin, right in the middle of it, Jesus still died for me. The Bible does not say to wait until we are perfect and then try to get right with God. No—Jesus says He came for sinners. The healthy do not need a doctor, but the sick do.

He has removed our sins as far from us
as the east is from the west.

—*Psalm 103:12*

Something inside me broke. All the pain from so many years poured out in tears streaming down my face, filling the pages of that Bible. I began to break down while I read about how God loved me—how He loved me so much that He sent His Son to die for me, for everyone! That God could forgive me for everything I had done. That He wishes that none should perish but that all should repent and turn to Him. That He *will* forgive me. I'd known this when I was younger, but after all I had done and the hurt I had caused, I questioned if He really could forgive it all. I was still skeptical that God could love someone like me after how far away I had gone from Him. But reading the words that explained how He loved and forgave me regardless broke something inside of me.

First Steps into Feeling Forgiven

I wanted to feel like I could be forgiven, but I had severely damaged my self-worth. Years of living for myself did not satisfy me or give me the peace and freedom I was looking for. It bound me in so many chains that I felt like I was drowning and trapped. Sin has natural consequences. When we live outside of the covenant of God, we are also outside of His protection and the promises in the Word. When we do not follow His ways (and even when we do), bad things hap-

pen because we live in a fallen world. The Bible talks about sin looking good for a season, but in the end, it is the road to destruction. The sense that I was enough—or even worth anything after all I had done—was hard to understand and accept, but I wanted to.

How could a perfect God ever love someone like me? A voice constantly screamed in my head, telling me I was *trash, worthless, dirty,* and *unforgivable.* I now know that it was not God's voice at all. It was the enemy that comes to steal, kill, and destroy. Allowing this voice to spew lies into our lives can change our perception of ourselves and make us feel unredeemable. Listening to it keeps those chains tightened around us, and we are unable to break free. But with God's help, we have the authority to silence that voice.

There is a major difference between condemnation and conviction. Condemnation is from the enemy. Condemnation is that awful voice that says, "Hey—what you did? That's unforgivable. How can God ever love you after that? You might as well give up and keep doing what you're doing because you are a worthless lost cause." Conviction is from God. Conviction is that soft voice that says, "Hey—what you did? That was not okay. Come to me, and I will forgive you, heal you, and help lead you so that it doesn't happen again." Both voices may not always be pleasant. The voice of conviction is meant to bring you closer to God, while condemnation is a tactic of the enemy to pull you away from God. We must not confuse the two.

I continued to read more of the Bible, not really know-

ing why. I just knew it made me feel better. Later, I learned that reading the Word of God is like washing out all the old ways of thinking. It renews our thoughts and minds. For me, years of lies had to be replaced with God's truth and who God calls me. He calls me *worthy, loved, priceless, beautifully made*, and *formed for a purpose*. This is what He calls all His creation: "It is good!"

I made up my mind that I was going to give "this thing" a try. I was not even sure what "this thing" was, but I knew anything was better than where I was right then. My first step was to stop drinking. I would not go out and party—not that I had anyone to go with. It was the last semester of my senior year of college, and I was still alone. I reached out to my family more during this time because I was still isolated from everyone else around me.

A New Life

One day, I got a call from my mom. She called and said, "There's this guy…" <*Insert eye roll here.*> Normally, I would never entertain the idea of meeting (let alone go out with) a guy my mom suggested. I did pretty well on my own, or so I thought. But I gave in and agreed to meet this man. It turned out he would become my husband and the wonderful father of my three beautiful boys. It still amazes me how God has His hand in everything, working all things for my good.

How Dennis and I met is a testimony in and of itself. His mom and my mom worked at the same middle school. With a PhD in biochemistry, his mom was overqualified for her

position as a small-town middle school science teacher. Dennis had been laid off from his engineering job, and his heart had been broken over the end of a long-term relationship. Instead of letting him sit and wallow in his misery, his mom told him to pick himself up and had him come to her classroom. Dennis went with her to school each day and helped the kids who had a hard time reading. My mom watched this tall, tan, handsome young man walk into the school every day, and her mind went right to setting us up. But first, she had to butter him up. She made him cookies and banana bread before mentioning, "So, I have this daughter...".

I was reluctant when I got the call from my mom: "There's this guy..." But after stalking his Facebook pictures and seeing that he was, in fact, a tall, tan, handsome young man, I agreed to let our moms exchange our numbers.

We began our relationship by texting non-stop and finally agreed to meet for our first date on St. Patrick's Day. The date started off rocky. The poor guy was so nervous he couldn't look me in the eye for the first two hours. When I pulled out my Batman wallet at the restaurant, his inner nerd was a little less intimidated. We talked and laughed for hours after that. Dennis will tell you that the moment he saw my Batman wallet, he knew he was going to marry me.

Things started to get a little better. Bit by bit and piece by piece, I felt like I was starting to pull the shattered pieces back together again, but I could only do so much on my own. I graduated with my nursing degree and moved back home to be closer to Dennis. We quickly moved in together, got two

dogs, bought a house, and got married, all within the span of two years. Things moved fast for us. During this time, we did not have a relationship with God. We did what we felt made us happy. We both grew up in Christian homes, so we claimed to be Christians, but we didn't live up to the standards of the Bible. We were not attending a regular church. We were not reading the Word, praying, or growing in our faith. We lived how we wanted to live. I fell into old habits and ways of acting because while I knew God was real, I still did not have a personal relationship with Him to help me heal all the things I needed to have healed.

I was drinking often and would make a fool out of myself in front of Dennis' friends and family. I struggled with my self-worth and often tried to push Dennis away, but he never left. No matter how ugly it got, he loved me through all the hard times. Though I had someone I knew who cared for me, I did not have peace in my heart. I struggled with thoughts of self-harm, lustful thoughts, feelings of worthlessness, and unforgiveness for myself and others. I knew I was not living in a way to please God, but I thought it was okay—at least I wasn't as bad as I was in college. I was beginning to work on my relationship with God, but I didn't really know Him or care if what I was doing hurt His heart. But then, everything changed.

Going Deeper with God

Less than two months after we were married, I found out that I was pregnant. Not with just one baby, but twins.

(I feel like the Lord got a little chuckle out of this. If you think you can do things in your own strength, have twins—it will give you a quick understanding of your need for the Lord!)

When the boys were a little over a year and a half, we started attending His Tabernacle Family Church in Ithaca. At first, it was just a favor to my parents and out of a sense of moral obligation. You are "supposed" to go to church when you have a young family, take the kids, let them go to Sunday school and learn all the cute Bible stories. I didn't think that church was something I needed or would get much out of. But as I sat there on our first Sunday (my arms crossed and eyes rolling), I began my journey of coming to know Christ more. It helped that His Tabernacle is not just a church but a family that loves people and preaches the powerful Word of God, not just a preacher's opinion. It's a church that wants its people to be knowledgeable and empowered, so it offers trainings, classes and opportunities for growth. The church teaches correct theology and biblical principles such as forgiveness, healing, Holy Spirit power, blessings, and seed time and harvest. It is about a relationship with God and not just a religion. No wonder its vision is "Loving God, Saving Souls and Developing Leaders." It truly wants its followers to know God and to make Him known.

I learned a lot in such a short time there, and many weights lifted off me. Chains I had been carrying for so long were broken. I learned that I could be fully forgiven for all my past sins, not because of anything that I had done, but

because of what Christ did for me. I was learning to let go and be free from so many titles and labels that the world had given me. *Victim, failure, liar, cheat, hopeless, thief, addict—* none of those labels were mine anymore. I learned I am a child of God. I learned that I was adopted into a new family and was given a new identity. I didn't have to listen to the lies of the enemy labeling me. I was learning to renew my mind with God's words about me, to hear His voice and to have a relationship with my creator. I was learning ever more deeply that my God loves and values me so much that He sent His son, Jesus, to take away all my pain and condemnation.

Conviction Over Condemnation

God first had to help me with forgiving myself. I felt guilt and shame associated with my past and a familiarity with the voice of the enemy speaking condemnation into my life. The Holy Spirit uses conviction as correction. He will reveal areas in our lives that do not align with the Word of God, not to shame us, but to get us to change and come to Him. Conviction helps restore our relationship, while sin separates us from a relationship with God. God is holy, and therefore He cannot tolerate sin. When we choose to sin, we choose to distance ourselves from God. The Holy Spirit uses conviction to turn us from that sin and bring us back into a relationship with Him.

> *Now repent of your sins and turn to God, so*
> *that your sins may be wiped away. Then times*

*of refreshing will come from the presence of
the Lord.*

—*Acts 3:19–20*

Conviction pushes us to turn to God to be forgiven and refreshed, but condemnation is different. Condemnation shames and makes us feel hopeless, as if we could never be forgiven for our actions. It wants us to move farther away from God and His forgiveness. These are lies and tactics used by the enemy. We can become accustomed to hearing condemnation from that inner whisper, and it can start to feel like reality. We start to believe the lie that we have gone too far, done too much and that God could never forgive it all.

But God is not intimidated by our sins.

The Bible says that when Jesus died, He conquered hell, death, and the grave. He was victorious over it all, and His blood washed away the sins of the world. Do our sins have more power than the sacrifice and the blood of Jesus? No!

*But if we confess our sins to him, he is faithful
and just to forgive us our sins and to cleanse
us from all wickedness.*

—*1 John 1:9*

God promises to forgive us, but we also must forgive ourselves. We must see ourselves with the value that God sees us as having. When we accept Jesus as our Lord and Savior, we no longer live out of our sin consciousness but out of

Christ's righteousness. All past shame is washed away, and God sees us as His children, not because of the good works we try to do but because of the finished work of Christ on the cross.

Change did not all come at once for me. After about a year of going all-in—reading the Word, taking classes, praying, worshiping, and spending time with God—with God's help, I was able to stop drinking. Even after becoming a mom, I had still been a heavy drinker. I would have a few glasses of wine every night to feel a sense of peace. I told myself that the wine was just a way to calm myself down and deal with the daily stresses of life. Then, one night at a young adults' service, God asked me, "Why do you drink?" I answered that drinking allowed me to relax and have some peace. He replied in the most loving way, "I will be your peace that passes all understanding if you let me." God revealed I was using drinking as my god and trying to fix everything with it. I learned God will not share His throne with anyone or anything else. I had to let God be the only god in my life. When I stopped drinking and gave my dependence on alcohol over to the Lord, He was able to start healing me. To this day, I have not had the desire to drink. I was free and healed from that dependency and instead chose to depend on God to be my peace. The thing I used to numb my pain all those years was now eliminated.

By stopping drinking, I was allowing God access to reach into other areas of my life. It started a domino effect of allowing God to search me and touch other not-so-obvious

areas of hurt in my life that He had been waiting to deal with. Remember, God is a gentleman and He will not go to places where we do not allow Him in. I have heard it explained like a house. When you have people over, you allow them access to common areas—the living room, dining room, kitchen, and bathroom. Maybe if they are family, they might be allowed into your bedroom or basement, but we all know there is at least one area where *no one* is allowed. Maybe it's the messy closet we haven't straightened up in years or that embarrassing junk drawer. Some places mortify us—we want no one to see them. Those are the places in our hearts that God wants access to. He wants it all, but He won't go there unless we give Him permission. We have to be willing to give God that permission, and when we do, He is able to help and heal like no one else can.

The Process of Forgiving Others

The next issue God wanted to help me with was my unforgiveness toward those who had wronged me. I had a bad relationship with one of my older sisters. When I was in high school, she used the situation that happened to me in my family's home to try to tarnish my parents' reputation. I was so hurt I told her I no longer saw her as my sister. I didn't want to be a part of her life, and I didn't want her to be a part of my life, either.

I completely cut her off and out of my life for about eight years before I began attending His Tabernacle Family Church. Then one day, my sister showed up at a Sunday morning

service. I ignored her and acted like she wasn't there, which wasn't easy because few people were in attendance. I was still angry at her for the things she had done and the ways she had hurt my family in the past. I didn't think she deserved forgiveness, and I didn't want a relationship with her.

She continued to come to services, and I continued to ignore her for months until an amazing woman of God, Pastor Rhonda Spencer, had a conference in which she preached based on the message in her book *No More Hurt*. (If you have not read this book, I assure you: it is life-changing!) She explained how unforgiveness is a sin that separates us from our relationship with God and all His plans for us here on Earth. Unforgiveness is like a cancer that can eat away at our bones. The unforgiveness that we have for someone has no effect on them. It only hurts the one with the unforgiving heart. It's like drinking a bottle of poison and expecting it to hurt someone else. I had never heard this perspective before.

After her message, I was still stubborn, as we all can be sometimes. I didn't want to let go of the hurt my sister had caused my family. She never apologized for what she did. I didn't want to forgive her: I didn't think she deserved forgiveness. But then I heard from God: "Did you deserve to be forgiven for all the things you have done? No, but I forgave you anyway."

I realized that forgiving my sister was just as much about me letting things go as it was for her. My unforgiveness was a choice I was holding on to. Forgiveness is a will, not an emotion. We will not always feel like forgiving. As Christians, we

should not live out of our feelings, but "by my Spirit, says the LORD" (Zechariah 4:6). Forgiveness is an act of obedience in response to what God did for us. For my healing, I realized I needed to let go of my hate for her. If I did, I would be giving God another weight that I would not have to keep carrying. It was *my* choice to make. I did not need her to say that she was sorry. I did not need her to change. *I* needed to change and let it go. Again, I will say forgiveness is a choice, not a feeling. My own heart was the only thing I could control in this situation, anyway—that and what I would do with my unforgiveness.

The next Sunday, my sister approached me in church. I prayed to see her through God's eyes and not through the lens of my hurt. A flood of compassion came over me. I was finally ready to let it all go; I was exhausted from hating her. I started crying, hugged her, and told her I had forgiven her. I was not saying what she did was okay, but I no longer wanted to carry hate toward her. I needed to forgive her for me, just as much as for her. It was not easy, and we did not become instant best friends. Sometimes, boundaries are needed in relationships to be healthy. Healing can take time, and there is an ongoing process, but forgiving someone I carried such hate against for so long was freeing.

It began preparing me for what God had next.

No Longer a Victim

I make known the end from the beginning,
from ancient times, what is still to come. I
say, "My purpose will stand, and I will do all
that I please."

—Isaiah 46:10 NIV

God is outside of time. He knows the beginning from the end and all the parts in between. I am amazed at how each step in my story happened exactly as it did and was perfectly timed.

About a year after my relationship with my sister was restored, I was still going to His Tabernacle, learning more about God and drawing closer to Him all the time. One night, I got an odd text from my mom asking if we could talk. Usually, she just calls me, so her text raised an eyebrow. I went to my bathroom for privacy and called her. She began talking with me about going out to dinner with a woman from our church who had been away for some time. This woman had asked my parents out to dinner. She wanted to talk with them and have her boyfriend come, too.

My parents happily agreed to have dinner with her and her boyfriend. But when she arrived, she was alone. She explained her boyfriend could not make it—and she was pregnant. She shared that she wanted to return to church but was afraid she would be judged. She and her boyfriend wanted to get married and to have Jesus be the center of their lives again.

Her boyfriend's name was Dean.

Yes, *that* Dean.

I dropped to the floor in my bathroom when my mom revealed that detail. One would expect my first reaction to have been panic, disgust, fear, anger, worry, or hate… but it wasn't. It was joy! I was immediately flooded with overwhelming feelings of peace, hope and unexplainable joy.

My mom learned from the woman that Dean had been to prison, but that is where he had his first encounter with God and His love and forgiveness there. He was living and working near Ithaca and already had a son, whom he loved dearly. The woman shared how much Dean loved his son and that his actions as a father were what initially drew her to Dean.

Tears streamed down my face as I listened.

All those years of regret, fear, anger, nightmares, wondering what happened to him, wondering if he was in jail or dead—all the questions were answered. I was thankful to

know that God had been working in his life just as much as He had been working in mine. I was fully convinced: there is *nothing* God cannot do! He can turn *all* things for good. I saw God could not only heal and take care of me but that God watched over Dean, too and loved him just as much as He loved me. God is no respecter of persons. No sin is too great for God to forgive.

While hearing the person who hurt you is doing well might not cause many to feel joy, it brought me joy and peace. If I had heard about Dean even two months earlier, I don't think I would have had the same thoughts, but God had healed something inside me. I was free, and I had forgiven him.

That victim was gone!

I saw three images flash, one after another, as real and as vivid as the page you are reading: me hugging Dean; a glimpse of this book; Dean and I on a stage talking to others about this story and what God can do.

I sat on my bathroom floor weeping out of joy and awe over how awesome God is. I kept repeating, "That is so freaking cool! God is so good! You can't tell me God isn't real and doesn't have His hand in all of this." Nothing had happened yet, but I knew God would get the glory. That's called the gift of faith, and it was so strong. I knew that God would turn this whole thing around for our good. He would redeem the years of hurt and pain and turn them into joy and peace.

Mom and I cried and laughed on the phone. She said she would go out to dinner with Dean the next week. I asked her

to make him feel loved, welcomed, and forgiven—because that is what he was. "And please," I said, "invite him to church."

I wanted to meet with Dean before he came to church to avoid any awkward "Capri-revelation moment-slash-breakdown" in the back row again like I had with my sister, but that was not how it happened. It took just one Sunday to change everything.

***

I was serving in the church on the worship team while my husband was running sound and media. I was still new to the worship team and very nervous. One Sunday morning, I was asked to lead a worship song for the first time, and the pastor asked me to give my testimony in service about how God had helped me stop drinking and changed my life. I shared how I was like the lost sheep that God left the 99 for to come and find.

It also happened to be the very Sunday that Dean came to visit the church for the first time. (Talk about God working!)

Service ended. I was taken aback by the presence of God in that service and in awe of His goodness when I decided it was time. I walked over to where Dean sat. I wasn't nervous—I felt totally at peace. I looked him straight in the eyes. I didn't see the boy who had hurt me. I saw the man who God loved.

I choked out some sort of "Hello," and then before I knew it, I hugged him.

Dean cried and shook and kept saying, "I am so sorry."

I told him, "I forgave you a long time ago. I am proud of you and the father I've heard you've become. I'm so excited for you and your new little one on the way." I continued, "God is awesome! I could forgive you, not because *I'm* that good of a person, but because God has already forgiven *me*."

We hugged and cried until both of our kids stole back our attention.

Healing and peace came from this brief but long-overdue exchange. I felt so lucky that I had finally gotten the answers to my questions over the years and that God allowed me to see His amazing plans for our lives. To paraphrase a favorite song of mine: When we can't see it—God is working. When we can't feel it—God is working. God is always working!

My life has never been the same since that day.

***

Dean and his family continued to attend our church for a time. I witnessed the whole family's baptism and saw changes in their lives.

While his family no longer attends our church, I often pray for them. I have seen how amazing my God is and how much He cares. He has never left me or forgotten even the tiniest detail of my life, and I believe God will continue to work in their life. God knows every pain and heartache and has all the power to help overcome any circumstance. He is my victory!

My New Story—Healed and Whole

Since that day, God has done so much in my life. My husband went to Bible college and completed his degree in ministry. Four years later, he left his job as an engineer and pursued his call to ministry full-time. With lots of guidance, amazing teachers, and divine preparation, we were given the honor of becoming the head pastors of the His Tabernacle Ithaca campus. It still amazes me how God works. Obedience yields an accelerated harvest. God had amazing plans for my life, but I could not step into that next level until I was obedient to forgive. I had to be willing to surrender and give God my YES!

God healed so much brokenness for me through that one act of obedience. It amazes me that I no longer harbor any anger in my heart towards Dean. The years of hurt, fear and anger are gone! I can't even see him as the same boy who hurt me. When I tell the story now, it feels like I'm telling someone else's story—that's how deeply God healed me. It's not that I mentally deny what happened; I simply no longer experience any pain associated with the memory. That is what God can do! That is the complete healing that He has for you, too.

> *"I have seen what they do,*
> *but I will heal them anyway!*
> *I will lead them.*
>
> *"I will comfort those who mourn,*
> *bringing words of praise to their lips.*

May they have abundant peace, both near and far,"
says the LORD, who heals them.

—Isaiah 57:18–19

"The Lord who heals them." That phrase is powerful to me. He is the God who forgives and heals. It is what He wants for us all! He wants us to have peace and joy. There is such freedom in forgiveness.

To all who mourn in Israel,
he will give a crown of beauty for ashes,

a joyous blessing instead of mourning,
festive praise instead of despair.

—Isaiah 61:3a

I felt bound for so long. Once I was able to let go and let God help me forgive, I finally experienced joy again. I was able to be at peace. I no longer subconsciously wondered if one day I would have to face this giant again. It was done. I was free! I traded in my bitterness and fear and received God's promises.

What Will Your Story Be?

This does not have to be just my story. Healing can be yours as well. You do not have to do anything alone!

My flesh and my heart may fail,
but God is the strength of my heart

and my portion forever.

—Psalm 73:26 NIV

I could never have forgiven Dean on my own. Forgiveness does not come naturally. It is supernatural, and that is why we need a supernatural God. Only He helps us heal and enables us to forgive. But forgiveness is a choice. We get to choose to forgive or choose to hang on to pain, anger, and regret. I'm thankful God is our strength in all of this.

You may think, *Okay, Capri, it sounds easy for you, but you don't know my story. You don't know what I have been through. You don't know the pain I have, all the nights I cried myself to sleep, the times I tried to forget or fix it on my own with no success. You don't know what they did to me or said to me or about me.*

And you are right. I do not know, but God your Father does. He knows. He has seen every tear you have cried, every pain and hurt you have felt. He was there through it all. He was there, and He wants to help take the shame, the anger, the pain, and the hurt away.

> *You keep track of all my sorrows.*
> *You have collected all my tears in your*
> *bottle.*
> *You have recorded each one in your book.*
>
> *—Psalm 56:8*

He collects every tear. God loves you dearly and completely. He cares deeply for you and does not want you, His

beloved, to go on hurting. Let me gently warn you: keeping the pain you have locked away from Him will slowly but surely destroy you and the plans God has for you.

Before dying on the cross, Jesus looked out into the crowd over all the people who had just ordered His execution, though He had never done anything wrong. He looked out over all the people who beat Him, spat on Him, ripped out parts of His beard, cheered as He was whipped so much that He didn't even resemble a person anymore, applauded as He stumbled to that hill carrying the cross on His beaten body, mocked Him as He hung on the cross, nails pierced through His hands and feet, gasping for every breath. Our beautiful, loving Savior looked at them and said, "Father, forgive them, for they know not what they do" (Luke 23:34, ESV).

That was his dying request—*Forgive them.*

If Jesus endured all that and still forgave, so can we.

See, Jesus was not just talking to people in that crowd. He was also talking to you and me. He looked through all of time, knowing who we are, knowing that we would fall short and sin. Jesus looked at you and asked the Father to forgive you. He loves you so much that He was willing to come and die a terrible death on the cross for you.

Prayer for a Lost Child to Come Home

Right now, you can take that first step in healing. You can allow God to come into your life and accept a relationship with Him as your Savior and Healer. It does not matter what you have done or whether you think you are worth it.

Jesus thought so, and He died for you.

You can pray this prayer wherever you are:

Dear Jesus,

I believe that You are God and that You came and died for me to be saved and made whole. I believe You rose again. Forgive me of all my sins, and help me to forgive others. Come into my life and make Yourself real to me. Wash me and cleanse me. Heal all my brokenness and help me know that I am a child of God. I am saved, and I am made whole today. I am born again and a new creation in Christ. In Jesus' name, amen.

If you prayed that prayer, the Bible says that all of heaven is rejoicing because a lost child just came home! I rejoice right along with heaven.

Now, get ready for a wild ride! God's plans for your life are amazing, even if they are not always what you expect. He wants to take you to places you never thought possible, which means facing things you never dreamed of dealing with, things that felt so deep and dark that the light could never touch, but that is God's specialty—He is the God of the impossible.

So, What Is Next?

Since you have read my story and have seen that it is possible to receive healing despite being deeply hurt and to forgive despite being terribly wronged, I want to share some practical and biblical applications for your life. Your story may or may not be similar to mine, but you have heard it, and something in you stirs with the desire to be free from the bondage of unforgiveness. The following questions can help start a journey toward healing and wholeness.

- How do we stop being victims and live how God calls us?
- How do we start the process of forgiveness?

#1: Start with God's plan

...Anyone who belongs to Christ has become a new person. The old life is gone; a new life has begun!

—*2 Corinthians 5:17*

When we accept Jesus as our Lord and Savior and choose to follow Him, we become children of God. As children, we need guidance on how to live our new life in Christ. We need to draw close to God and learn His ways because, ultimately, He is the only one who can truly help.

> *My old self has been crucified with Christ. It*
> *is no longer I who live, but Christ lives in me.*
>
> —*Galatians 2:20*

When we accept Jesus as our Savior and Lord, we acknowledge the following: *It is not my will, but yours, Lord. My ways of doing things are dead and gone. I have been crucified with Christ.* The things we have tried to do to save ourselves in the past have not worked, but God's ways are higher than our own. He has all the answers, and we need to replace our thoughts with His.

How? Through daily Bible reading.

Daily Bible reading changed my life. How can we ever know God if we never read what He made for us? All His words, thoughts, and plans are in His Word, clear as day. When I hear people say, "God works in mysterious ways," I recognize that they don't truly know God. He is not mysterious—He is consistent. The Bible says time and time again, "I am God, and I do not change." His plans for us are all written there—peace, joy, love, prosperity, health, and forgiveness. Reading the Word daily replaces thoughts that cloud our minds with truth.

I struggled for a long time with negative self-worth. I would literally hear internal voices telling me that I was *worthless, ugly, fat trash* and that no one cared if I was alive or dead. When I came back to Christ, those voices didn't automatically go away; it took time for me to recognize the voice of the enemy versus the Voice of Truth. The truth is that you are loved, you are precious to God, you are worthy of saving and of love, and nothing you can do can ever separate you from God's love. The Holy Spirit's voice must be the loudest one in your head as you move toward healing and a relationship with Him. We need to quickly identify the voice of the enemy and take the authority to compare that voice with the truth found in the Word of God. But if we are not reading the Bible, we will not know what it says and will be left without the weapons that we need to combat the schemes of the devil.

The ways of God are found in love, compassion and forgiveness.

> *The LORD is compassionate and merciful,*
> *slow to get angry and filled with unfailing*
> *love.*
>
> *He will not constantly accuse us,*
> *nor remain angry forever.*
>
> *He does not punish us for all our sins;*
> *he does not deal harshly with us, as we*
> *deserve.*
>
> *—Psalm 103:8–10*

The more I learn about God and grow in my relationship with Him, the more I see that time and time again, God is faithful. He is patient, and He is always willing to forgive. When we repent and turn away from sin, God will not bring up the past to condemn us. The Bible says that He removes our sins as far as the east is from the west (Psalm 103:12), and He remembers them no more.

Now, just because God forgives does not mean there are no natural consequences for sin. The consequences of our words and actions in this world are very real. There are many nights that I do not remember what happened because of blackout drinking. I don't remember things I said, places I went, or what I did with whom. These are consequences I live with. I could be sitting in church on a Sunday, and someone from my past could walk in, but I might not even know it. I have to live with the trail of hurt I caused others while selfishly trying to make myself feel better. I have friendships that have not been restored and trust that is still broken.

Sin has natural consequences, but thank God we now live under grace. We can use our past to testify to God's goodness and share how He fixes brokenness. Many people have told me that they have seen how God has radically transformed my life, and they know that if God could transform my life, He can do it for them as well. I will never try to hide my past because it is just one part of my story, and it shows the goodness of God. God can take all that the enemy meant to use to destroy us and use it for His good.

For God was in Christ, reconciling the world to himself, no longer counting people's sins against them. And He gave us this wonderful message of reconciliation. So we are Christ's ambassadors; God is making His appeal through us.

—2 Corinthians 5:19–20a

God calls us to be His hands and feet, representing Him to a lost and dying world. Knowing that God is patient, loving and forgiving, how can we show God to others if we cannot forgive? If God does not remember our sins, why would we continue to bring up another person's? We need to learn to forgive as Christ forgives.

#2: Choose to forgive because God forgave us

Can I challenge you?

God has already paid for the sin of the person who hurt you. That terrible thing they did to you or someone you love? God will forgive them if they turn to Him and repent.

You may say, "That is unfair! They should be punished for all the hurt and pain they caused." But does God punish us for the pain we cause others by our sins? Jesus taught that we need to remove the log from our own eye before we go after the speck in another's eye (Matthew 7:5). In my own story, just as He forgave me of all my sins when I turned from them and repented, He forgave Dean's when Dean turned back to Him.

This revelation was huge for me. God loves the person I hate the most and died for him. God does not distinguish between varying degrees of sin. He does not have a scale in heaven where He weighs one sin worse than another. As imperfect people, we make moral judgments about varying degrees of sin. But God just sees sin, sin that separates us from Him. God hates the sin, but He loves the person.

He is just and willing to forgive us of all our sins (1 John 1:9) if only we will turn away from them and follow Him. He has already made a way for us to be forgiven. How can we, as children of God, think someone does not deserve to be forgiven?

> *You have heard the law that says, "Love your neighbor" and hate your enemy. But I say, love your enemies! Pray for those who persecute you! In that way, you will be acting as true children of your Father in heaven. For He gives His sunlight to both the evil and the good, and he sends rain on the just and unjust alike. If you love only those who love you, what reward is there for that? Even corrupt tax collectors do that much. If you are kind only to your friends, how are you different from anyone else? Even pagans do that.*
>
> *—Matthew 5:43–47*

It is against our flesh to forgive, but when we live out of the Spirit, not out of the flesh, it is possible. If we are new creations, we can have the mind of Christ, and we can learn to forgive, no matter what. If we claim to be God's children and know He has already forgiven those who have sinned against us, how can we not forgive them, too?

When we hold onto unforgiveness, what do we do? Essentially, we hold onto the accusations of another person's sin. That sounds like "the accuser of the brethren" who "accuses them day and night" from Revelation 12:10. The scripture is about Satan. When God dropped that perspective on me, it stung—but it was also helpful for me because the last thing I want to be compared to is Satan. I want to be like Christ—therefore, I need to forgive like Christ. I need to forgive *all*.

Consider the story of Joseph. His brothers hate him and plot to kill him but decide instead to sell him into slavery (what a nice family, right?). He is sold as a slave in Egypt and then is put in jail after false claims of rape are brought against him by his master's wife. If anyone could be "justified" in their unforgiveness, he could! But if we read the whole story, we see God use the awful things people do to Joseph to perfectly position him to be in place to help save the whole region, including his family and brothers who sold him. Can you imagine if he held onto his unforgiveness and decided not to be used by God? Instead, Joseph chose forgiveness as the best revenge.

Dear friends, since God loved us that much, we surely ought to love each other. No one has ever seen God. But if we love each other, God lives in us, and his love is brought to full expression in us.

—1 John 4:11–12

God loves *all*! I'll say it again to let it sink in—God hates sin but loves the person.

This is a hard concept to accept if we have never experienced God's love. If we have never experienced His forgiveness, how could we understand why He wants us to forgive, just as we have been forgiven?

I love the story in the Bible about the "immoral" woman who washes Jesus's feet with expensive perfume and her tears.

I tell you, her sins—and they are many— have been forgiven, so she has shown me much love. But a person who is forgiven little shows only little love.

—Luke 7:47

The woman pours out her love for Him while humbling herself at His feet. She is so thankful for being forgiven that she pours all she has at the feet of her Savior. She understands that nothing she's done can separate her from Christ's love. The experience of forgiveness changes our lives so deeply we can never look at things the same way again.

I identify with the woman who washes Jesus' feet in many ways. My sins were many, but my amazing God forgave me. He didn't look at me as a lost cause, so how can I look at any of his other children as too far gone for forgiveness? Our capacity and willingness to forgive others is directly correlated with our experience and understanding of Jesus' forgiveness for us.

I now am more aware of areas where I harbor unforgiveness towards others. There will always be hurt and people who hurt us, but we can recognize that we do not have to hold on to that hurt. We can remember that God forgave us, so we can also be quick to forgive.

The scripture I share next will be the last in this section on choosing to forgive. It was convicting to me, and I still work on it daily.

> If someone says, "I love God," but hates a fellow believer, that person is a liar; for if we don't love people we can see, how can we love God whom we cannot see?
>
> —1 John 4:20

If you're like me, you may need to meditate on it for a while. I promise it's worth it.

#3: Don't hold on to hurt—give it to God

When someone speaks or does something hurtful to you or someone you love, it can leave a wound that cuts deep.

Every time you think about that event, the pain from that wound can grow down deeper if you have not forgiven the one who left you wounded. That wound can then turn into what the Bible calls a root of bitterness.

> *Look after each other so that none of you fails to receive the grace of God. Watch out that no poisonous root of bitterness grows up to trouble you, corrupting many.*
>
> —Hebrews 12:15

"A root of bitterness" refers to pain, resentment, or an attitude towards a person or God that results in a separation from being able to hear truth or receive correction. This root of bitterness can become a poison that makes it impossible to accept or hear God's truth. When we hold onto hurt, we can justify our unforgiveness. Pride can take over and unforgiveness can own us. It becomes a slippery slope that can trap us in a cycle of hurt where it feels like there is no way out. But the blood of Jesus has provided a way out.

> *You have come to Jesus, the one who mediates the new covenant between God and people, and to the sprinkled blood, which speaks of forgiveness instead of crying out for vengeance like the blood of Abel.*
>
> —Hebrews 12:24

God is a merciful, loving God who comes with forgiveness, not vengeance. He wants to help us have that heart as well. He sees your deepest pain. He knows and He understands. This is the hurt that God wants to take from you. Consider the interaction between Jesus and the man with leprosy (a painful disease).

> *Suddenly, a man with leprosy approached him and knelt before him. "Lord," the man said, "if you are willing, you can heal me and make me clean."*
>
> *Jesus reached out and touched him. "I am willing," he said. "Be healed!" And instantly the leprosy disappeared.*
>
> *—Matthew 8:2–3*

Jesus instantly healed the man of his physical condition. God is able to take away all hurt (physical or emotional), and He wants to do so. He is able and willing.

He is not only a God of the small things. He wants to be the God of our big things, too. He is the only one with the power to heal and not just medicate.

I know it is hard to forgive. Sometimes forgiveness is challenging because we are deeply wounded, and we have carried hurt for so long that it feels like it is simply a part of who we are. Also, we may have been taught that we don't have to forgive. As a result, many hold on to unforgiveness their whole lives. Society has normalized it by glorifying the act of

cutting people out of our lives rather than dealing with the issues that led us to that place. It took time for me to develop enough of a relationship with God to help me heal and remove the layers of hurt, pain, anger and a need for revenge. Because I was holding onto them so tightly, I was stopping myself from moving forward and healing. When I learned who God is, that He is a God of justice but also grace, I learned to be still and know that I can trust my loving Father to take care of me. I could finally let go and give my pain to Him.

> *And the peace of God, which transcends all understanding, will guard your heart and your minds in Christ Jesus.*
>
> —*Philippians 4:7 NIV*

When I first came back to Christ, I did not understand how I could ever change or how God could forgive me and help me heal, but that's the awesome thing about God. He can do it even without me understanding it. We don't have to understand it all, but God is able. Even if we can't understand it with our worldly minds, we can still stand and be confident that He can heal us—that is faith.

> *And do not be conformed to this world, but be transformed by the renewing of your mind, so that you may prove what the will of God is, that which is good and acceptable and perfect.*
>
> —*Romans 12:2 NASB*

This world would have us believe that if we forgive someone, we are letting them off the hook and that they do not have to pay for what they have done. But the Lord says, "Vengeance is mine, I will repay" (Romans 12:19 ESV). We are not the judge and jury; the Lord is. We must believe that He will bring justice. His justice may look very different from the world's standards, but that is why God is God, and we are not.

I am thankful to serve a loving, forgiving, and just God. He knows and wants what is best for us. He has been doing this for a long time and will continue to do so. I will trust in His wisdom and ways over my own.

If your heart has been holding unforgiveness, anger, and hurt, then that root of bitterness that we spoke about could be something you have been facing. This deep root can cause such an injury to your heart, and if your heart has been injured, it needs to be made whole.

> *Get rid of all bitterness, rage, anger, harsh words, and slander, as well as all types of evil behavior. Instead, be kind to each other, tenderhearted, forgiving one another, just as God through Christ has forgiven you.*
>
> *—Ephesians 4:31–32*

A new heart is only given by Jesus through His unfailing love and forgiveness.

> *Moreover, I will give you a new heart and put a new spirit within you; and I will remove*

the heart of stone from your flesh and give
you a heart of flesh.

—*Ezekiel 36:26 NASB*

Jesus makes all things new. He will take your brokenness and make it new. He will take your relationships and make them new. He will take what the devil tried to destroy and make it new. Jesus let you loose; now let it go.

He [Jesus] gave up his life for her [the church]
to make her holy and clean, washed by the
cleansing of God's word.

—*Ephesians 5:25b–26*

Your healing can start through reading this book. I include many scriptures throughout the chapters because the Word of God washes away the thoughts and labels of this world with the truth of the Word. The Bible says that when the Word is sent out, it does not return void (Isaiah 55:11). It will accomplish what it was sent out to do. You can be healed of your hurt right now. He is Jehovah Rapha—the Lord that heals.

#4: Don't try to do it alone

You may be thinking, *I want to forgive; I just don't know that I can on my own.*

There is a phrase in the Book of Zechariah that reveals we must lean on God for what we can't do on our own: "'Not

by might, nor by power, but by my Spirit' says the LORD" (4:6). Forgiveness is not natural. As humans, we do not innately want to forgive. It takes a supernatural God to help us. Only He can.

The key is the Holy Spirit.

The Holy Spirit is not a *what* but a *who*. He is the third person in the Holy Trinity: God the Father, God the Son, and God the Holy Spirit. Most people believe that because the Holy Spirit is spoken about as the third person, He is in some way in third place and, therefore, a lesser part of God. But that is the furthest thing from the truth.

The Holy Spirit is all God—just as God the Father is all God and God the Son is all God. They are three, yet one. Don't worry if you are hearing this for the first time and it is hard to understand. Many seasoned Christians also have difficulty fully comprehending the Trinity.

What you need to know is who the Holy Spirit is to you. He is the Helper, the Counselor, the Comforter, and the *power* to overcome.

> *But the Helper, the Holy Spirit, whom the Father will send in my name, He will teach you all things, and bring to your remembrance all things that I have said to you.*
>
> —*John 14:26 NKJV*

Holy Spirit is our teacher and the one who can help and even correct us when needed. Jesus said it would be better

that He go to heaven because then the Holy Spirit can come and be with us. He reminds us of what the Word of God says.

> *May the God of hope fill you with all joy and*
> *peace in believing, so that by the power of the*
> *Holy Spirit you may abound in hope.*
>
> —*Romans 15:13 ESV*

That last part is the most important—He provides the power. Often, when we see ordinary people do extraordinary things in the Bible, it is not because they willed themselves to change and do something supernatural. No—the Holy Spirit empowered them to do so.

Consider Peter. He is Jesus' disciple who denies knowing Jesus not just once but three times because he faced the threat of persecution. Skip forward just a bit. In Acts chapter 2, Peter leads 3,000 people to Christ in one sermon in the very same city that was filled with people who were in the crowd crying "Crucify!" and were responsible for putting Jesus to death. He goes on to heal many, preaches the gospel to the Jews amidst persecution and ends up dying for his faith as he proclaims that Jesus is the Savior of the world. You cannot tell me he just decided to change his ways and boldly proclaim the gospel in the midst of certain bodily harm—no, it was the power of the Holy Spirit.

Acts 2 describes the day of Pentecost when all 120 of Jesus' closest followers are in the upper room, a sound from heaven comes like a mighty rushing wind and tongues of

fire settle on everyone in the room. In that moment, the Holy Spirit comes upon all, and they begin to speak in other tongues as the outward sign of the inward change and the power they now possess. Holy Spirit now comes to do this life with you each and every day—leading, guiding, correcting, empowering, comforting, teaching, renewing, and strengthening. He has many amazing attributes, but He is an absolute gentleman. He will not come where He is not invited and welcome.

If you have accepted Jesus into your life as your Lord and Savior, then you have experienced the saving power of God. Your eternity is secure—but what about life here on Earth now? We live in a fallen world—but our good Father does not leave us helpless and powerless. He gives us the Holy Spirit, who can dwell on the inside and lead and guide us.

The same Spirit that lives on the inside is the Spirit that raised Jesus from the dead. Any unforgiveness we harbor is not too hard for the Holy Spirit.

> *But you will receive power when the Holy Spirit comes on you; and you will be my witnesses in Jerusalem, in all Judea and Samaria, and to the ends of the earth.*
>
> *—Acts 1:8 ESV*

The *power* Jesus is talking about is the word *dunamis*, which means "miraculous power, miracle," and "mighty working power." When the Holy Spirit comes upon us, He

gives us that power to overcome, including the power to overcome hurt and the power to forgive.

Receiving the baptism of the Holy Spirit gives us the power to overcome. The baptism of the Holy Spirit is a free gift available to all who believe. We simply have to ask for it. It is as simple as praying this prayer:

> *Jesus, you are the baptizer of fire and of the Holy Spirit. Baptize me now in the name of Jesus. Give me the power to forgive and overcome hurt.*

The Holy Spirit can even give you the power to pray for those who hurt you. Wow!

> *But to you who are willing to listen, I say, love your enemies! Do good to those who hate you. Bless those who curse you. Pray for those who hurt you.*
>
> *—Luke 6:27*

When we let go of hate, anger, and pain and instead pray for God's will and blessing for a person who wronged us, we are truly living how the Word tells us to. God's plan and desire for us is complete forgiveness and healing.

***

These four practical keys—following God's plan, choosing to forgive, letting go of hurt, and relying on the Holy Spirit—are just the beginning of the journey of learning to

forgive. Forgiving others is not a one-time event. Situations come up daily where we need to check our hearts, go to God, and ask Him to help us forgive someone.

People will offend, lie, and gossip; we will be hurt by others. Sin is all around us because we live in a fallen world. But our job is to forgive quickly so that offense and bitterness do not take root. It is our job to humble ourselves, ask God to help us with our hurt, and allow Him to soften our hearts to forgive others. In the end, unforgiveness can separate us from our purpose, healing, relationships and even God.

> *And so, dear brothers and sisters, I plead with you to give your bodies to God because of all he has done for you. Let them be a living and holy sacrifice—the kind he will find acceptable. This is truly the way to worship him. Don't copy the behavior and customs of this world, but let God transform you into a new person by changing the way you think. Then you will know God's will for you, which is good and pleasing and perfect.*
>
> *—Romans 12:1–2*

Don't let the poison of unforgiveness take you out. Forgive quickly!

> *Don't let evil conquer you, but conquer evil by doing good.*
>
> *—Romans 12:21*

You Are Victorious

But you belong to God, my dear children.
You have already won a victory over those
people, because the Spirit who lives in you is
greater than the spirit who lives in the world.

—1 John 4:4

You have the victory already when you are attached to the one who has victory over all. It does not matter if you can see the end from the beginning because God can. He knows exactly how things are going to work out, and He will be able to turn everything for good. He cannot control our decisions or our free will, but He can use the decisions that align with His will if we choose to start following Him. We must turn from what we used to do and the decisions we used to make and submit our will to God's will. We cannot expect God to continue to fix our messes if we willfully continue to disobey God. This is like saying *God, you can fix this broken glass, but then I'm going to throw it and shatter it again, and I expect it to be fixed over and over again.* He can fix it because He is God, but it would be far better if we stopped throwing the glass in the first place. Natural consequences for our actions will always exist. God has a better plan for our lives than we could ever have, so we need to trust Him, turn 180 degrees from what we were doing and let God be God.

So, let go and let God be the Lord over your life and in every situation.

> *Do not be afraid or discouraged, for the LORD will personally go ahead of you. He will be with you; he will neither fail you nor abandon you.*
>
> —Deuteronomy 31:8

God's Plan for Your Life Is Victory

You are God's beloved child. He is the creator of the whole universe—He wants nothing less for you than overwhelming peace and joy. Jesus came to this Earth to live as a man. He experienced all the same hurt and pain that we do, such as rejection from friends and family, lies and insults, and He was persecuted, although He never did anything wrong. He had many chances to be offended and harbor hate and unforgiveness—but He didn't. He knew that it would only lead to destruction.

God knows what you are going through—but He gives you the power to overcome and live in victory.

> *But you will not even need to fight. Take your positions; then stand still and watch the LORD's victory. He is with you, O people of Judah and Jerusalem. Do not be afraid or discouraged. Go out against them tomorrow, for the LORD is with you!*
>
> —*2 Chronicles 20:17*

The Lord is with you. He will help and guide you. Nothing is impossible for Him. No hurt is too big or too small for Him. God will help you fight the battles in your life. Whatever you are dealing with, especially if it is unforgiveness, stand still and stand firm. Choose to not be offended.

> *I chose to hear nothing*
> *and make no reply.*
>
> *For I am waiting for you, O LORD.*
> *You must answer for me, O LORD my*
> *God.*
>
> —*Psalm 38:14–15*

We do not have to even acknowledge when others wrong us. We can have peace and freedom when we choose to forgive even little offenses. This feeling is literally contagious! When I found out I didn't have to hold onto the hurt others caused me, it was freeing. I learned that when we find our-

selves hurt, we can stop, look at the situation and recognize that we are operating out of offense. The Holy Spirit will convict us. This conviction can serve as a quick reminder that we need to forgive because of how crippling unforgiveness can be. We have the power of the Holy Spirit to forgive any offense.

> *No, despite all these things, overwhelming victory is ours through Christ, who loved us.*
>
> —Romans 8:37

"Despite all these things," as Paul wrote to the Romans, God can rewrite your story and take you from victim to victor.

God did it for me, and He can do it for you. I am no one special. Like I told Dean—I am not a super good person or super saved—I just believe the Word of God is true and that all things are possible. Healing is possible. Forgiving your enemy is possible. Praying for those who hurt you is possible. Your story can be rewritten. God is waiting for you to take the first step, choose to believe Him, and ask Him for help. He loves using those who think they are unqualified to bring Him glory. Your story can bring God glory, and you can be someone else's answer! Your story of healing and victory in spite of pain could be the answer someone else needs.

Forgiveness Does Not Mean Relationship

I don't want you to think that I am saying that the outcome of your story has to look like mine. You may never get the chance to face the person who hurt you. The person who hurt you may have passed away, is still trying to hurt you, isn't a safe person to be around, or has no interest in ever being a part of your life.

You do not need to have an encounter with a person to have an encounter with God.

You can experience healing and forgiveness through Christ while keeping healthy, safe boundaries. That is called wisdom, and the Bible talks a lot about it. Forgiveness may be given, but that does not mean trust is automatically also given. Forgiveness is required, but trust is earned. God does not ask you to put yourself back into the same situation with someone who hurt you. Sometimes, for the safety of all involved, setting boundaries and keeping your distance are the best ways to love someone. Your story is no less miraculous if it doesn't have the type of ending mine did. There is still a huge testimony if you forgive that person alone in your room late at night. It can be between you and the Lord as He speaks to you, inviting you to let Him begin healing your wound as you forgive.

Your Story Can Change Others

Your story can impact others around you. It may be just what others need to hear to stir their faith for their miracle.

The Bible describes a woman with an issue of blood in the books of Matthew, Mark, and Luke. In that time and culture, menstruating women were considered unclean and not allowed to be out in society. She has suffered from bleeding for 12 years, and she believes that if she can touch the hem of Jesus' garment, she will be healed. Despite the threat that she could be put to death for being in a public place, let alone touching another person, she pushes her way through a crowd to get to Jesus. Because of her tenacity, faith, and belief that suffering is not her portion, she knows that all she needs is to get to Jesus, and she will be made well. Because of her bold action, she becomes a public testimony and a faith-builder for another person in the crowd.

A man in the crowd named Jairus is a leader in the synagogue and likely knows the woman. He may have sentenced her to a life of solitude because of her condition. He has the authority to put her to death simply because she has entered the public space, but he is dealing with his own faith crisis. His daughter is dying, and he is in the act of pulling Jesus with him to his house to have Jesus heal her when this woman with the issue of blood breaks through the crowd and, by her faith, causes Jesus to stop and heal her.

The moment he witnesses the miracle of the woman who has suffered for 12 years being healed, Jairus gets the most earth-shattering news of his life. A servant from his home comes and tells him his daughter has just died. When Jesus overhears the news, He says, "Do not fear, only believe" (Mark 5:36, ESV).

I wonder if the tenacity of the woman with the issue of blood who was healed strengthened Jairus's faith to believe for the miracle he needed for his little girl?

Spoiler alert—Jesus raises her back to life. (Isn't God good?)

Sometimes, your healing and your testimony will be the catalyst that someone else needs to get theirs.

It's Time to Praise Him!

I encourage you: make a scene about all the Lord has done for you.

Think about the story of Paul and Silas praying in jail (see Acts 16:16–40). After they are thrown in prison for preaching about Jesus, their praise shakes the very jail where they are being held. The shaking then sets all the jail's captives, not just Paul and Silas, free. When the Roman soldier supposed to be guarding them thinks they are all gone, he plans to kill himself. But when he finds everyone is still there and witnesses the awesome power of God, he, along with his whole family, is saved.

That is already an amazing story of how God can use the seemingly worst of situations and turn them for good—but then the Pharisees realize that they have done wrong by beating and imprisoning Paul and Silas. They want Paul and Silas to leave quietly and not make a scene, but Paul and Silas will not. They know their rights. They know their citizenship and the promises they are entitled to. They do not want to leave quietly. They want it to be known publicly that the Pharisees

are wrong and that what they tried to use to harm them is a testimony of what God can do with a terrible situation to turn it for good. God works what the enemy intends for bad, for their good. So, make a scene about the goodness of God in your life! Testify the goodness of God and allow Him to get all the glory.

***

God is ready to start this journey with you. Lean on Him, trust in Him, and He will guide you through life's ups and downs. He is your victory, your strength and your peace through all of life's storms. You are no longer a victim but victorious through Christ Jesus.

> *Don't worry about anything; instead, pray about everything. Tell God what you need and thank him for all he has done. Then you will experience God's peace, which exceeds anything we can understand. His peace will guard your hearts and minds as you live in Christ Jesus.*
>
> *—Philippians 4:6–7*

Afterword—
My Prayer for You

If you have read this far, I want you to know I am proud of you. This book is not only about my testimony but also a workbook that you can take and apply to your life.

I pray that this book presents the truth of the gospel, that people will hear it, and that they will accept Jesus as their Lord and Savior. I also pray it will help Christians struggling with hurt and unforgiveness find freedom in Christ.

I pray the Holy Spirit talks to you and reveals past or current hurt you are dealing with and works on your heart to help you let it go and give it to God.

I pray the label of *victim* has been broken off and that you accept the truth of what God calls you and take on your new nature as a child of the King, as an heir with Christ Jesus.

I pray you have the courage to share your story of how God has worked in your life.

If this book has impacted you, I would love to hear about it. Please feel free to reach out and share your testimony of what God has done. I would be delighted to celebrate with you how great our God is. Email me at:

pastorcapri@histabernacle.com.

I pray that God keeps your heart softened to His love and correction. I pray you are strengthened to live a victorious life and take off the victim label in all areas. I pray your story has been changed in only the ways that He can change you.

You are loved and have such a purpose here on this Earth. I pray you complete all God has for you with joy and empowerment from Him.

You are not a victim; you are victorious through Christ Jesus!

www.ingramcontent.com/pod-product-compliance
Lightning Source LLC
Chambersburg PA
CBHW031001090426
42737CB00008B/628